Tudor
Exploration

Moira Butterfield

FRANKLIN WATTS
LONDON • SYDNEY

First published in 2010 by Franklin Watts

Copyright © Franklin Watts 2010

Franklin Watts
338 Euston Road
London NW1 3BH

Franklin Watts Australia
Level 17/207 Kent Street
Sydney NSW 2000

A CIP catalogue record for this book
is available from the British Library.

Dewey number: 910.942'09031

ISBN 978 0 7496 9594 1

Printed in China

Franklin Watts is a division of Hachette Children's Books,
an Hachette UK company.

www.hachette.co.uk

The text of this book is based on *Focus on Tudor Life: Tudor Exploration*, first published in 2006 by Franklin Watts.

Designer: Jason Billin
Editor: Sarah Ridley
Art director: Jonathan Hair
Editor-in-Chief: John C. Miles
Picture research: Diana Morris

Note to parents and teachers:
Every effort has been made by the Publishers to ensure that the websites in this book are suitable for children, that they are of the highest educational value, and that they contain no inappropriate or offensive material. However, because of the nature of the Internet, it is impossible to guarantee that the contents of these sites will not be altered. We strongly advise that Internet access is supervised by a responsible adult.

Picture credits
AGE/Superstock: 14.
AKG Images: 22.
Ashmolean Museum/University of Oxford/Bridgeman Art Library: 18.
Nancy Carter/North Wind Pictures: 4b, 26.
Corporation of London/HIP/Topfoto: 23.
Mary Evans Picture Library: 19, 27.
Guildhall Art Library/City of London/Bridgeman Art Library: 28.
Kunsthistorisches Museum, Vienna/Bridgeman Art Library: 16.
Metropolitan Museum, New York/Bridgeman Art Library: 15.
Derek Middleton/FLPA Images: 10.
The National Martime Museum, London: 5t, 6, 8, 12, 13.
Louie Psihoyos/Corbis: 21.
Joel W Rogers/Corbis: front cover, 1, 9t, 17, 29.
Service Historique de la Marine, Vincennes/Bridgeman Art Library: 3t, 25.
Shawn Spencer-Smith/matthew.co.uk: 7.
The Tate, London: 24.
Wellcome Library, London: 11t.
Adam Woolfitt/Corbis: 20.

Every attempt has been made to clear copyright. Should there be any inadvertent omission please apply to the publisher for rectification.

Contents

Finding the world

Tudor kings and queens ruled England from 1485 until 1603, a period of time sometimes called the Age of Exploration.

Silks and spices

At the beginning of the Tudor period, Europeans knew very little about the rest of the world — only what they were told by merchants who travelled to Europe from places such as China and the Far East. These merchants became very wealthy by charging lots of money for unusual foreign items such as silks and spices.

We want your wealth

The monarchs of Spain, France, Portugal and England could see how rich the eastern merchants were, and they

Key fact

A Venetian called Marco Polo journeyed to China in the 13th century and returned with amazing stories of emperors and treasures. His tales made other Europeans want to explore.

Spices such as peppercorns (back), nutmeg (front left) and cardamom (front right) sold for huge prices in England.

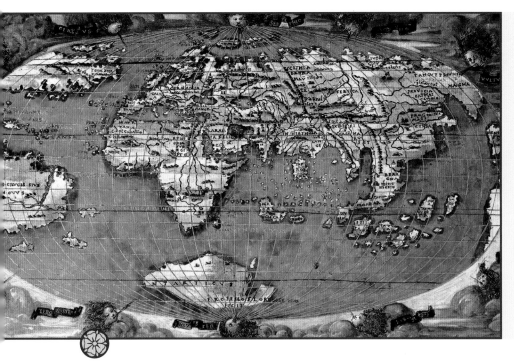

Go and visit

The National Maritime Museum in Greenwich, London, is the world's biggest maritime (seafaring) museum. It has lots of exhibitions about ships and true-life ocean adventures.

This map of the world dates from early Tudor times. It does not show much of North or South America.

wanted that wealth for themselves. They sent ships to areas where no European sailors had been before, to find new goods to sell in Europe.

Indian adventure

The Portuguese were among the first to sail far away from Europe. Their ships were the first to go around the southern tip of Africa, and the Portuguese explorer Vasco da Gama and his crew became the first Europeans to sail to India in 1497–98. It was a tough journey though and only 60 of his 180 sailors returned alive.

Did you know?

Another Portuguese explorer, Ferdinand Magellan, is said to have made the first voyage around the world, between 1519–1522. In fact he was killed part of the way round but one of his ships, the *Vittoria*, eventually returned to Spain with news of the journey.

5

Go west!

European sailors were keen to find a quick sea route to the Spice Islands of south-east Asia, where most of the spices grew.

Quicker by sea

The spice merchants used to travel overland from the Spice Islands and had to pay customs duty (a tax) on their goods in all the countries they passed through. Europeans realised they could make more money themselves by sailing straight to the Spice Islands (also called the East Indies), to buy the spices and ship them home to sell.

Accidentally to America

Sailors in early Tudor times thought that they could find a short cut to the Spice Islands by sailing west across the Atlantic Ocean. They didn't realise that North and South America were in the way, because no complete maps of the world existed.

Did you know?

In 1497 John Cabot was given £10 by Henry VII for discovering the "new-found land". He set off on another expedition in 1498 but was never heard of again.

In September 1492, the Italian Christopher Columbus set out on a voyage paid for by King Ferdinand of Spain. He landed in the Bahamas, in the Caribbean, which he claimed for Spain, followed by other parts of Central America. In 1497, John Cabot sailed west from England on behalf of Henry VII, and discovered what he called the "new-found land", now part of Canada.

Cabot's original ship, the Matthew, *was a small light ship called a caravel.*

Go and visit

In 1997 Cabot's ship the *Matthew* was reconstructed to retrace Cabot's voyage. You can sometimes visit it in Bristol harbour, where the original ship began its journey.

Ships improve

Up until Tudor times trading ships sailed around the coasts of Europe without ever going too far out of sight of land.

Better ships

Sailing the open ocean was more difficult than coastal sailing, and needed a stronger type of ship. Spanish and Portuguese shipbuilders designed a sailing ship called a carrack, with a deeper hold (storage space) for supplies and goods.

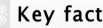

Key fact

This picture shows a carrack. You can see its three masts and its flat stern, which has a rudder attached to it.

Go and visit

At the National Maritime Museum in Falmouth, Cornwall, you can find out all about sailing ships. You can reach the museum by ferry, and also sail to a nearby Tudor fort built by Henry VIII to guard against foreign invasion.

New look for ships

Before Tudor times medieval ships were pointed at both ends and were steered by a large oar which hung over one side. On a carrack the steering oar was replaced by a giant piece of wood called a rudder attached to the stern (the back) of the ship. The stern was made flat instead of pointed, to fit on the rudder.

Did you know?

The right-hand side of a ship is called the starboard side. This is because the steering oar (also called the steere-board) always used to be on the right-hand side.

Strong and smart

A carrack had a strong wooden body that could survive a battering from ocean storms. It was made of planks fixed onto one long timber, the "keel", that ran along the length of the hull like a backbone. It had three masts, with square sails on the front and middle masts and a triangular sail on the mast at the back. Older ship designs had fixed sails but carrack sails could be swung around to catch the wind whichever way it blew.

A tough trip

Explorers set sail with no idea what they would find and no hope of rescue in an emergency. They worked in awful conditions.

Small for sailors

In Tudor times ships were very small compared to modern ones. John Cabot's ship, the *Matthew*, was only 20 metres long and six metres wide. It sailed across the stormy Atlantic with a crew of just 18. Such a small crew would have had to work very hard to control the ship on the voyage.

Salt and maggots

There was no refrigeration on a Tudor ship, and the only way to keep food from rotting was to soak it in salt, so sailors lived on a

Key fact

The *Matthew* took seven weeks to sail across the Atlantic. Luckily, there were so many fish in the sea that the sailors were able to catch some just by lowering baskets into the water.

Rats infested ships in Tudor times. They ate the sailors' food supplies and sometimes gnawed through ropes.

Go and visit

The *Mary Rose* in Portsmouth. It sank in 1545 but was raised in 1982. You can see the sailors' belongings, found near the wreck, and find out about life on a Tudor ship.

boring diet of salted meat. They also ate ship's biscuit, a type of bread made from flour and water and then baked hard. The salted meat often went off and the ship's biscuits became infested with maggots and beetles.

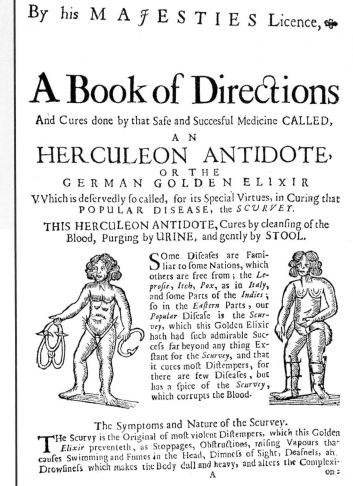

By his MAJESTIES Licence,

A Book of Directions

And Cures done by that Safe and Succesful Medicine CALLED,

AN

HERCULEON ANTIDOTE,

OR THE

GERMAN GOLDEN ELIXIR

VVhich is deservedly so called, for its Special Virtues, in Curing that POPULAR DISEASE, the *SCURVEY*.

THIS HERCULEON ANTIDOTE, Cures by cleansing of the Blood, Purging by URINE, and gently by STOOL.

Some Diseases are Familiar to some Nations, which others are free from ; the Leprosie, Itch, Pox, as in Italy, and some Parts of the Indies ; so in the Eastern Parts , our Popular Disease is the Scurvey, which this Golden Elixir hath had such admirable Success far beyond any thing Extant for the Scurvey, and that it cures most Distempers, for there are few Diseases , but has a spice of the Scurvey, which corrupts the Blood.

The Symptoms and Nature of the Scurvey.

The Scurvy is the Original of most violent Distempers, which this Golden Elixir preventeth, as Stoppages, Obstructions, raising Vapours that causes Swimming and Fumes in the Head, Dimness of Sight, Deafness, and Drowsiness which makes the Body dull and heavy, and alters the Complexion :

A

Scurvy

Many sailors of the time died from a terrible illness called scurvy, caused by not eating enough Vitamin C, which is found in fresh fruit and vegetables. These foods were not available on a voyage far from land, and nobody understood why scurvy struck anyway. It caused swollen gums, rotting teeth, bruises, bleeding, madness and eventually death.

Did you know?

Lots of useless cures were suggested for scurvy, such as the ones listed on the poster above. But the true cure — eating food rich in Vitamin C — was not discovered until the late 1700s.

Finding the way

The sailors of the Tudor age would have recognised their local coast, but on the open ocean they had to find new ways to work out where they were.

Minus a map

There were no reliable maps for the explorers to use, since many of the places they came across had never before been visited by Europeans. Map-makers were only able to start drawing accurate charts when the explorers returned with information on what they had found.

Equipment such as this astrolabe helped early seafarers to find their way. It helped them to work out the ship's latitude — its position north or south of the equator.

Which way now?

Sailors used a magnetic compass (right) to work out directions on their voyage. It contained a magnetic needle which always pointed north. They also used a measuring instrument such as an astrolabe (left) or a cross-staff, to measure the position of the sun or the stars in the sky. They could use this information to work out how far north or south their ship was (its "latitude").

The Queen's pirates

By the middle of the 1500s Spain had become an enemy of England, because England had turned away from the Catholic religion and Spain was strongly Catholic.

Stealing from Spain

Spain claimed ownership of the lands Christopher Columbus discovered in Central and South America. They discovered the fabulous treasures of the Aztec and Inca empires, as well as gold and silver mines, and they started to ship the treasure home. Queen Elizabeth I heard of the new Spanish wealth and wanted some of it for England, so she gave English sailors an official licence to attack Spanish ships in return for a cut of the treasure they stole.

A treasure made from South American gold.

Official pirates

Elizabeth's licensed pirates were called privateers. Whilst on their search for Spanish riches to steal, they got used to sailing across the Atlantic and around the coasts of the "Spanish Main", as the Spanish

Did you know?

Once a year the Spanish sent a fleet of a hundred ships, called galleons, home from the Spanish colonies, carrying treasure from its gold and silver mines.

A portrait of Christopher Columbus. He claimed many lands in Central and South America for Spain.

colonies (settlements) in America were called. They got more and more experienced at sailing the open ocean, and began to discover new lands for themselves.

Adventurers abroad

Sending sailors across the Atlantic as privateers was a cheap way for Queen Elizabeth to fight the Spanish.

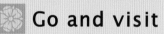

Key fact

Spain melted down a lot of silver and gold from its new colonies, to make coins. Silver coins were called "pieces of eight".

Go and visit

Buckland Abbey in Devon was the home of famous Elizabethan sailors Sir Francis Drake (see page 16) and his cousin Sir Richard Grenville. Drake is said to haunt the grounds.

It was also a way to make some money and find new places where England could set up her own colonies. But Spain was very angry, and executed any privateers they could catch.

Drake around the world

Sir Francis Drake is the best-known English sailor of the Tudor age.

Sailing against the Spanish

Drake was born in Devon. He and his cousin John Hawkins sailed to the Caribbean to make money by trading, and went on raids against the Spanish. His voyage around the world was planned as another stealing trip, and he set off with five ships and 164 men in 1577. By the time he sailed round the southern tip of South America he only had one ship, the *Golden Hind*, and 58 men left.

Did you know?

Sir Francis Drake was a pirate, an explorer and a national hero, whose tactics against the Spanish Armada in 1588 saved England from Spanish invasion.

All the way around

On his journey Francis Drake raided Spanish settlements in Peru and Chile and captured Spanish treasure ships. Then, because he thought Spanish ships might be chasing him, he carried on sailing west through the Spice Islands, bought lots of spices and sailed on home to Plymouth. His voyage took three years.

Voyage of death

During the trip Drake and his crew had to survive on penguin and seal meat as they sailed around the tip of South America. Some sailors died of disease; others from the cold. Four of the ships in his fleet were destroyed or forced to sail home, but the trip eventually made Drake very wealthy, and on his return he was given a knighthood.

Key fact

The 37-metre-long *Golden Hind* seems very tiny to have made such a long journey. Yet when Drake returned, it contained the modern-day equivalent of about £25 million worth of treasure!

Go and see

A full-sized reconstruction of Sir Francis Drake's ship the *Golden Hind* is moored in Brixham, Devon. Climb on board and find out about the incredible world journey the ship made.

The route north

By the mid-1500s, European sailors knew that there were routes to Asia around southern Africa and the tip of South America. They wanted to find a northern route, too.

Trying but failing

The northern route from the Atlantic Ocean to the Pacific Ocean is called the north-west passage. Elizabethan privateers and explorers tried hard to find it, but had no success because of freezing ice and stormy seas. In fact, no ship was able to sail through the north-west passage until the 20th century.

The search north-east

In 1553 ships led by Sir Hugh Willoughby and Richard Chancellor set off to find the north-east passage,

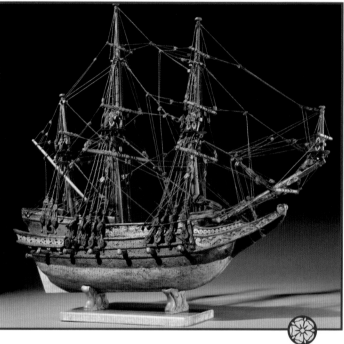

A model of an Elizabethan merchantman, a type of ship used by merchants and explorers alike.

Did you know?

Explorer Martin Frobisher brought back lots of stone from his trips north, believing it to contain gold. But the "gold" turned out to be worthless gold-coloured iron pyrites.

Key fact

Seagoing exploration was very dangerous, and many sailors died during their attempts to find new sea routes.

a route to China around the north of Norway. The expedition never found the short sea route they were looking for, and poor Willoughby froze to death with the crew of two ships. Their bodies were found a year later by Russian fishermen. Nobody sailed the north-east passage until the 19th century.

Tudor sailors voyaging in the Arctic faced the prospect of a cold death thousands of kilometres from home.

Go and visit

Visit your local sailing club. If you don't live on the coast or near a river, you might find a club at a reservoir or lake that offers lessons.

The slave trade

There was a big demand for slave labour in the new colonies, and so the slave trade grew.

Local misery

At first the Spanish settlers in South America used the local people to work as slaves, mining gold and silver or working on sugar cane plantations (farms). The Spanish treated them with great cruelty and saw them as little better than animals. Working and living conditions were so bad that many of them died, so new slaves were needed.

Manacles like these were used to chain the hands of slaves together, to stop them from escaping.

A human cargo

Men, women and children were captured by local slaving parties on the West African coast and sold to traders, who took them to the Caribbean. Here the Africans were sold as slaves in return for goods that could be taken home and sold for a profit.

Did you know?

Sir Francis Drake was one of the first English slave traders. Together with his relative, John Hawkins, he made money selling slaves to the Spanish.

Terrible trip

The African slaves were transported across the Atlantic chained together and packed below decks. Many died of starvation and disease onboard ship. Those who reached the Caribbean were forced by their new owners to work until they died. Slaves were not free to leave a cruel owner, were given no pay and only just enough food to survive.

This engraving shows African slaves packed together like items of cargo in a ship's hold.

Key fact

Today about 80% of the Caribbean community are descended from slaves brought over from Africa.

Go and visit

The Museum of Bristol. Find out how the slave trade grew after it was begun in Tudor times, what conditions were like for the slaves, and how the slave trade was finally stopped in Britain.

Home ports

London and Bristol were the two most important sea ports in England in Tudor times.

Paying for port

All the goods which came in to England from abroad had to be landed on official "legal quays" (areas where ships moored and unloaded). There the government charged the merchants customs duty (a government tax) on the goods. Anyone who landed goods secretly, without paying the tax, could be executed as a smuggler. Tudor ports were busy places. The picture of London on the right shows the River Thames crammed with shipping.

 **Did you know?**

Francis Drake's voyage was financed by a group of wealthy people who made a big profit. They got back £47 for every £1 they had invested.

Tudor merchants in London plan a voyage. They stood to make a lot of money, but there were also great risks.

Suppliers of ropes, sails and ships' supplies set up shop along the docksides. Sailors unloaded and loaded cargoes, or spent their wages in dockside inns.

Making money

Overseas voyages could make lots of money, but if a ship sank the people who owned it could lose everything. Groups of merchants and wealthy investors began to get together to form companies called joint stock companies, which put up the money for voyages and shared out the profits and the costs of disasters, too.

Go and visit

The Museum of London in Docklands, to find out about the London docks and discover what life was like in this important Tudor port.

Key fact

The success of the Tudor joint stock companies was the start of London becoming an important financial centre.

Sir Walter Raleigh

Sir Walter Raleigh was a favourite courtier of Queen Elizabeth. He helped found English colonies in North America, now the USA.

Raleigh rises

Sir Walter Raleigh came from Devon, like Sir Francis Drake (see page 16). He is said to have been out walking with the Court when he first impressed the Queen by laying his cloak in a puddle so that she would not have to step in the dirt. Nobody knows if this famous story is true, but Raleigh did have a picture of a cloak on his coat-of-arms (family badge).

This famous Victorian painting — The Boyhood of Raleigh — *by Millais shows the young Walter (left) listening to tales of the sea, and of new lands.*

24

Did you know?

Raleigh called the colony he founded in North America "Virginia" after Elizabeth, who was often called "the Virgin Queen".

Sending ships

In 1585 Raleigh sent five ships to North America loaded with people to set up a colony on the east coast. At first settlers were welcomed by the Native Americans, but soon there was fighting and the colony was destroyed.

This Elizabethan map shows the doomed colony of "Virginia".

Raleigh's fall

Raleigh upset the Queen by marrying without her permission, and she imprisoned him. When he was released he organised a voyage to South America. After Elizabeth died the new King, James I, became suspicious of Raleigh and he was again imprisoned and executed in 1618.

Go and visit

The Tower of London, where Raleigh was imprisoned. The second time he lived there for thirteen years.

Key fact

Raleigh became a hero in England because he helped to defend Devon and Cornwall from an invasion by the Spanish Armada in 1588.

Bringing home surprises

Tudor explorers brought back not just gold and slaves, but new foods which nobody had seen before.

Expensive treats

Spices from the Spice Islands, such as pepper and nutmeg, were highly prized. It was hard to keep food fresh in Tudor times, and the strong taste of the spices helped to hide the taste of stale and rotting food. Some of the spices were also used as medicine. For instance, nutmeg was used to treat stomach illnesses. Spices were very expensive, so they were mostly used only by wealthy people.

A scene in the Banda Islands, where nutmeg grew in Tudor times.

New food

Tobacco, potatoes, maize (corn on the cob), tomatoes and pineapple were introduced into England for the first time by explorers returning from the Americas. Sir Francis Drake brought back a coconut from his trip

Did you know?

A servant of Sir Walter Raleigh is said to have thrown water over his master when he first saw him smoking a pipe of American tobacco. He apparently thought Raleigh had caught fire!

This engraving depicts the tale of Sir Walter being "put out" by his servant.

around the world and presented it to Queen Elizabeth, who had never seen one before.

Tales of far-away lands

Tudor explorers brought back amazing tales of what they found. For instance, in the Spice Islands they had to dodge fierce head-hunting cannibals and in North America they had to fight man-eating polar bears. Some returning sailors wrote about what they had seen, but sometimes the tales sounded so strange that nobody believed them!

Key fact

Raleigh sent an artist called John White on the voyage of 1585. White painted images of Native Americans and of wildlife never before seen in Europe.

Go and visit

The Pitt Rivers Museum in Oxford, which displays weird and wonderful objects brought back to England from all over the world over centuries.

Exploration speeds up

By the end of the Tudor times Europeans knew a lot more about the world, thanks to the skill and courage of seamen such as Cabot and Drake.

British sailing power

Britain became expert at building ships and fighting at sea because of the lessons sailors learned attacking the Spanish or sailing the open ocean looking for new lands. Soon Britain had many new colonies abroad, and was making lots of money from them. It built up a powerful navy to protect them from enemies.

Queen Elizabeth visits the Royal Exchange in London. This was built by wealthy Sir Thomas Gresham in 1571 as a place for merchants to negotiate deals.

Key fact

The Tudor age ended with the death of Elizabeth I in 1603. She died childless, so the throne went to her relative James Stuart. The money she had made from exploration and privateering was all spent by the time of her death.

Merchants get rich

Before the Tudor period, only the nobles and the Church were rich in England. Their wealth came from owning farmland. But by buying and selling goods overseas, merchants began to get richer, and they eventually began to use their new-found wealth to get more power for themselves.

Did you know?

Elizabeth's successor, James I, sent ships — like the one shown above — to find out what had happened to the first settlers Sir Walter Raleigh had left in Virginia (see page 25). They found no-one.

Go and visit

Sherborne Castle in Dorset, a medieval castle rebuilt by Sir Walter Raleigh in 1594. When he was executed the castle became King James's property.

Glossary

astrolabe
An instrument used on board a ship to work out its latitude, its location north or south of the equator.

carrack
A three-masted cargo ship used in Tudor times.

colony
A settlement set up in a foreign land.

compass
An instrument used to navigate on a journey. It contains a magnetic needle that always points north.

cross-staff
A navigational instrument used for measuring the position of a ship.

customs duty
A tax paid to a government on goods that are brought into a country.

hull
The framework of a ship.

joint stock company
A group of people who paid for a ship's voyage, and then took a share of the profits or losses made by the venture.

keel
The large timber "backbone" that runs along the bottom of a wooden ship.

maritime
To do with the sea.

merchant
Someone who buys and sells goods.

navigation
Finding your way on a journey, by working out where you are and which direction you should go.

port
A town or city with a harbour where ships dock to load and unload.

privateer
A sea captain licensed by Elizabeth I to attack the ships and colonies of England's enemies.

rigging
The ropes used to control the sails on a sailing ship.

scurvy
A fatal disease which sailors suffered.

slave trade
The kidnapping of Africans who were taken to the Caribbean as slaves.

Spice Islands
The islands of south-east Asia, also called the East Indies, where spices grow.

spices
Aromatic plants and seeds used in cooking and medicine.

trade
The buying and selling of goods, such as spices and silk.

Tudor
The period between 1485 until 1603, when kings and queens of the Tudor family ruled England.

Timeline

1485 Henry Tudor becomes King Henry VII and the Tudor period begins.

1492 Christopher Columbus sets sail to find a route west to the Spice Islands.

1497 John Cabot sets sail to find a route west to the Spice Islands.

1497-8 Portuguese Vasco da Gama and his crew become the first Europeans to sail to India.

1509 Henry VII dies. His son, Prince Henry, is crowned King Henry VIII.

1519 Ferdinand Magellan of Portugal and his crew set sail to become the first crew to sail around the world.

1533-34 The English Church breaks with the Roman Catholic Church.

1547 Death of Henry VIII. He is succeeded by his son Edward VI.

1553 Edward VI dies and is succeeded by Mary I, his sister.

1558 Mary dies and is succeeded by Elizabeth I, her sister.

1576 Martin Frobisher sets sail to find a north-west passage to the Spice Islands.

1577 Francis Drake sets sail from England on a voyage that will end in him going all the way around the world.

1581 Francis Drake is knighted by Elizabeth I onboard the *Golden Hind*.

1585 Sir Walter Raleigh's settlers claim "Virginia" in North America for Elizabeth I.

1603 Elizabeth I dies. She is succeeded by James Stuart.

Websites

www.nmm.ac.uk
The website of the National Maritime Museum in Greenwich, London. Go to "kid's stuff" to find out all about being a Tudor explorer.

www.nmmc.co.uk
The website of the National Maritime Museum in Falmouth, Cornwall. Build a boat in an interactive game.

www.goldenhind.co.uk
See photographs of the reconstruction of Sir Francis Drake's ship the *Golden Hind*, and find out about life onboard.

www.maryrose.org
Find out about the Mary Rose exhibition. Take a virtual tour of the ship and meet the crew.

www.matthew.co.uk
See photographs of the reconstruction of John Cabot's ship the *Matthew*, and find out about its history.

www.museumoflondon.org.uk
Go to the learning section and then to the Tudor section for some fun activities and facts on Tudor life in London.

www.portcities.org.uk
Go to the Bristol section of the site to find out more about the slave trade.

Index